Kingdom of Longleaf

by Frances Kwiatkowski

for Kate & Liz

*and with many thanks to the talented
photographers whose work and generosity
made this book possible*

ISBN 9780692590607

Once upon a time, in a land of water and fire, a kingdom grew.
The kingdom was a majestic forest, full of air and light,
wiregrass and wildflowers, and the music of the wind in the
crowns of the trees- Longleaf pines. The kingdom was home
to many wild creatures and plants, some of which lived nowhere
else on earth, and some of whom created complex symbiotic
relationships with each other and with the landscape itself.
Long ago, the forest was so immense that it touched the
shores of two seas and covered almost 100 million acres…
but that was once upon a time…

Azures are small, pale blue butterflies that like open woodlands. Like many other animals sharing the Longleaf ecosystem, they have a symbiotic relationship with another species: ants. The ants protect azure caterpillars from wasps, and the caterpillars feed the ants a yummy secretion called "honeydew".

Azure, a pale blue star twinkles through the trees,
Glows against a sky of Longleaf green.
Delicate wings float and dip and flutter by,
Enchanted dance of the butterfly.

Bison once lived in the eastern U.S. Eastern wood bison (*Bison bison pennsyl-vanicus*) were larger and darker than Plains bison, with a smaller hump. They became extinct in the early 1800s.

Bachman's sparrow is a small bird only found in the southeastern United States. Known for its beautiful song, it lives in the open grassy areas of mature pine forests.

Bison graze in drifts under towering pines,
The herd ambles in long, crooked lines.
Bachman's sparrows dart, swoop, and follow along,
Whistling and trilling a Longleaf song.

"Candle tree" is a nickname for Red-cockaded Woodpecker cavity trees (trees they nest in). The woodpeckers drill small holes called resin wells around their nesting cavities. These holes drip resin, creating a sticky "wall" to keep out predators such as rat snakes. The resin looks like dripping candle wax, inspiring the nickname.

Candle trees drip sticky resin, amber sap,
Sign of a bird with a small red cap
Who pecks out a hole in a living pine tree,
Happily nests in this cavity.

Whitetail deer enjoy the Longleaf pine forest. In summer, they graze in the meadows and rest in the shade of the trees. In winter, the trees provide shelter from wind and weather. The white spots on a fawn's coat help him to blend in with the dappled shade of the forest floor, hiding him from possible predators while he sleeps.

Deer pause to rest from their early morning run,
Fawns curl asleep, dappled in the sun.
Does step silently on the pine needle floor
Then, graceful as dancers, turn... bound... soar!

Snowy egrets are beautiful, long-legged birds that nest and feed near water or wetlands. To catch fish, they stand frozen or take slow, stealthy steps through the water until a fish is unlucky enough to swim within reach. Then the egret quickly stabs the fish with its sharp beak and swallows it whole!

Egrets pose immobile on the sandy beach
Waiting for fish to swim within reach.
Patient statues watch for quick darts of silver,
Long leg lifts, and beak stabs the river.

Fire is to a Longleaf forest as Rain is to a Rain forest. Fire (started naturally by lightning strikes) keeps the understory of the forest clear of shrubs that would choke out grasses and young pines. Fire cleans up dead pine needles so that newly fallen pine seeds can reach bare soil. Longleaf pines have adapted in many ways to thrive in their partnership with fire.

Fire flickers orange, ignites with a spark
As summer lightning splits the dark.
Grasses flame hot to hurry the fire's race.
Tall pines are safe; thickets kept in place.

Gopher tortoises are a "keystone species" of the Longleaf pine ecosystem. This is a species that plays such a key role in a community that the survival of others depends upon it. The tortoise's large, roomy burrow creates a home for 250 other species! It is also a safe place during fires. Gopher tortoises live in only six states and are on the Endangered Species List.

Gopher tortoise digs a large hole in the earth,
A nice, dark burrow makes a snug berth.
Safe haven from fire or cold, deep underground,
He gives shelter to friends all around.

Hymns...
the music
created by the
wind blowing
through the
canopy of
Longleaf pines
has been
described as
a whisper in
the breeze,
a gentle
lullaby, and
the roar of
the ocean.
The explorer
William
Bartram
called it a
"solemn
symphony
of the steady
Western
breezes,
playing
incessantly,
rising and
falling through
the thick and
wavy foliage"
(Bartram,
110).

Hymns echo through the crowns of tall Longleaf trees,
Long needles rustle in symphony.
Tree music whispers and carries on the breeze,
Fades and swells in rhythm with the seas.

Indigo snakes are the longest native snakes in North America- they can grow to nine feet! Despite their huge size, they are extremely gentle and shy of people. They usually survive cold winters by curling up inside Gopher Tortoise burrows. Indigo snakes are named for the deep blue, or indigo, color of their scales. They are a Threatened Species due to habitat loss and the pet trade.

Indigo snakes are long, sleek, and number few.
Brilliant scales so black, they shine steel-blue.
She is graceful, gentle, and extremely shy;
Quietly suns beneath summer's sky.

Joe pye weed (*Eupatorium purpureum*) is a tall native wildflower. Clouds of pink-purple blooms appear in late summer and are loved by butterflies! Joe pye weed was once used by Native Americans as a medicinal plant and is named for a famous medicine man, Joe Pye.

Joe Pye Weed: tall and queenly meadow flowers,
Huge clouds of blooms, a bending bower.
Dusky rose petals, deep eggplant purple stems,
Sweet, late summer, subtly glowing gems.

Kingdom...
Once upon a time, the southeastern United States was a kingdom of Longleaf pine trees. Longleaf dominated the Piedmont and Coastal Plains of the southeast. The Piedmont region is a name for the foothills of the Appalachian Mountains. The Coastal Plain is land that was once the sandy floor of the Atlantic Ocean.

The Kingdom is...
Rolling meadow, a savanna for a sea;
A forest, the king of all: a tree;
Piedmont and coastal plain, born of sand and reef.
King of all: majestic pine... Longleaf.

Meadow...
the Longleaf
pine savanna
is fascinating
because it is
both a forest
and a meadow.
The pine trees
grow far
apart from
one another,
with meadows
of grasses and
wildflowers
growing in
the sunny,
airy spaces
between them.

Marsh...
the Latin
name of
Longleaf
is *Pinus
palustris*,
which means
"of the marsh".

Meadow and marsh weave wildflowers with grasses;
Bluestem with sunflowers, inkberry, liatris.
Pyxie moss, flameflower, coral bells twine;
Butterfly weed, sundew, passion vine.

William Bartram was the first American naturalist to explore, sketch, and write about the landscape of the southeastern United States. He was one of the first explorers to describe many plants, animals, and even Native American tribes to the rest of the world. His book, *Travels*, was published in 1791 and is still popular. Today, the Bartram Trail follows the route of his journey.

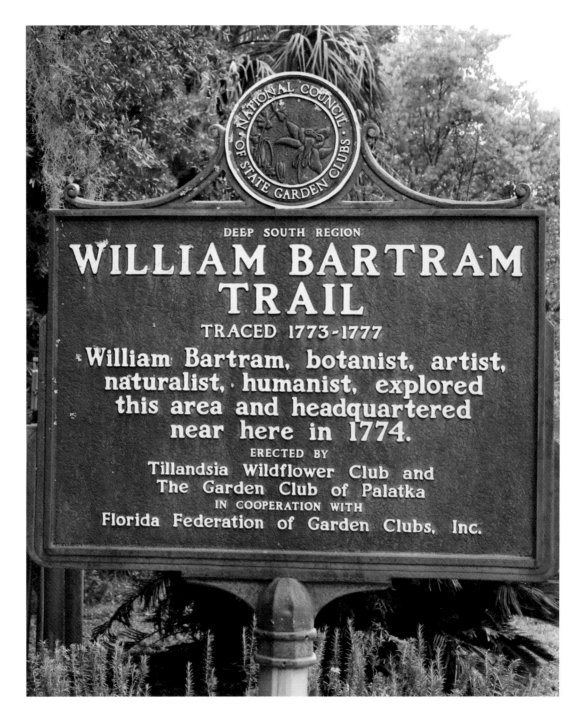

DEEP SOUTH REGION

WILLIAM BARTRAM TRAIL

TRACED 1773-1777

William Bartram, botanist, artist, naturalist, humanist, explored this area and headquartered near here in 1774.

ERECTED BY
Tillandsia Wildflower Club and
The Garden Club of Palatka
IN COOPERATION WITH
Florida Federation of Garden Clubs, Inc.

Naturalist William Bartram, first to see
(In year Seventeen Seventy-three)
And write of his travels through eight southern states
Of nature's beauty, both small and great.

Burrowing owls are quite unusual owls. Besides living in underground burrows rather than trees, they also stay awake during the day. These small owls often nest in burrows made by other animals, such as gopher tortoises. Baby owlets have an amazing defense against predators- they make a hissing noise that sounds like a rattlesnake!

Owls- tiny, long-legged, white-spotted and brown;
Owls that waken at dawn, not sun-down.
Burrowing owls that live and nest underground,
More thanks to tortoise, a new home found.

Pitcher plants (*Sarracenia*) are carnivorous plants- yes, they eat animals! Both unusually striking and beautiful, these amazing plants live in bogs or wetlands. Because their natural habitats are nutrient-poor, they obtain nutrients by trapping live prey such as flies, moths, wasps, ants, and sometimes even tree frogs!

Pitcher plants are striking, rare queens of the bog
Who trap and eat insects, flies, and frogs.
Jewel-bright blossoms of citrine and ruby,
Crystal flutes and bowls, not quite empty.

There are many varieties of pitcher plants. In most, the stalks of the plant resemble flowers, and they even secrete nectar to attract their prey. The lip of the stalk is slippery so that the prey easily falls into the pool of liquid at the bottom, and then digestive juices (like those in a person's stomach) dissolve it. Pitcher plants in the wild are precious and very rare. They are threatened because of over-collection and loss of habitat.

Bob-white
Quail
are named
for the
distinctive
call, "bob-
WHITE!"
They nest and
forage in the
native grasses
of open
woodlands.
If frightened,
quail will
freeze to hide
rather than fly
from danger.

Muscadine
is a
Southeastern
grape. The
thick-skinned
fruit is green,
bronze, or
dark purple,
and provides
food and cover
to wildlife.
People enjoy
them too!

Quail nest in the wiregrass and call "bob-white!"
Coveys freeze to hide, instead of flight,
In arbors of muscadine, thick-skinned bronze grapes;
Coral-fruit mayhaw, tasty escape.

Mayhaw trees grow in Southern wetlands. Mayhaw jelly is pale coral and deliciously sweet!

Red-cockaded Woodpeckers are the only woodpeckers to nest in living pine trees rather than dead ones. Named for the small red stripe or "cockade" on the males' heads, they are an endemic species of the Longleaf forest-- they live nowhere else on earth.

Red-cockaded Woodpeckers rat-a-tat tap
Wearing red feathers in tiny caps.
Families nest in clusters of living trees;
Another key, endangered species.

A savanna
is an open
grassland.
Longleaf pine
savannas
are a mixture
of grasses,
wildflowers,
and widely
scattered
pine trees.
Longleaf
savannas are
perhaps the
most diverse
ecosystem
in North
America.
170 plant and
animal species
can be found
in one quarter
of an acre.

Savannas, never still. Grasses swish and sway,
Shimmering, shining, an ocean's bay.
Rippling golden shadows on a summer day,
Humming with life beneath its green waves.

Tar and pitch were harvested from pine trees as early as 1715 to waterproof ships of the British navy. After the process of distilling turpentine from tree resin was invented in the 1830s, Georgia and Florida led the world in producing naval stores for over 100 years. By 1930, so many Longleaf pines had been harvested that 97% of the virgin forest was gone.

Tar and pitch, made long ago from kiln-burned trees,
Blackened hulls of ships on ancient seas.
Turpentine and rosin, made from flowing gum,
Life-blood of the pine drained for a sum.

The word "understory" refers to the plants growing below the canopy (or tree-top) layer of a forest. In a Longleaf forest, the open understory is a mosaic of various shrubs, wildflowers, and grasses. A Longleaf forest is home to around 900 plant species. This diversity is important for the animals that live in the forest.

Understory- sandy floor beneath the trees;
Its own, whole world, rich diversity.
A symphony of grass and flower species,
Nine hundred notes playing melody.

A vista is a distant view, especially one seen through a long passageway. Just imagine the view of a large, rolling, grassy meadow-- with grasses blowing gently in the wind, and wildflowers adding a splash of color here and there-- all framed by tall, elegant, and widely spaced pine trees. Gorgeous!

Vista- a view, a vision of gold and green
As far as one's eye or heart can see;
A dream of a forest, reaching wide and far,
Wide as the heavens, with trees for stars.

Wiregrass (*Aristida stricta*) is a keystone species of the Longleaf community. A perennial bunch grass, it is bright green in summer and vivid gold when dormant in winter. It is a dominant plant in the understory and provides food and cover for tortoises, birds, and mammals. Like Longleaf, wiregrass is both adapted to and dependent upon fire; it only flowers after summer fires.

Wiregrass- fine, airy sprays of stem and seeds;
Singing harmony, keystone species.
Food for the tortoise, and cover for the quail;
Burning fast, leads fire down the trail.

Wiregrass burns hot and fast, which encourages a forest fire to move quickly through the understory of the forest. This keeps the fire low and protects the tree canopy from the flames.

Xeric means "adapted to a dry environment." Longleaf can grow in very sandy and dry soils, as well as in wet, marshy areas- amazing adaptability!

Xeric- dry as the desert, sun-bleached bone.
Trees twist, stunted and bent, fully grown.
Dry sandhills, Piedmont plains, or wet coastal marsh,
Longleaf lives, adapts, survives the harsh.

Once upon a time, Longleaf pine forests covered 90 million acres, from Texas to North Carolina, and south to Florida. Today, America's Longleaf pine forest is less than two million acres. Conservation groups are working to preserve and expand the remaining Longleaf pine forest, a living national treasure.

Yesterday, the South was alive with pine-song;
Longleaf ninety million acres strong.
Forest of beauty and grace, a complex web
Of many lives caught in tidal ebb.

"Zebra-striped bird" is the Pileated Woodpecker, one of the largest in the U.S. Similar to the famous Ivory-bill, which may be extinct, Pileateds have black and white stripes on their necks, and scarlet, triangular crests on their heads. A mated pair will defend their forest territory (1000 – 4000 acres) by rapidly and loudly drumming their bills on trees.

Zebra-striped birds dart through pines and disappear,
Yet their drumming taps ring bright and clear.
May grasses burn so a forest will survive,
May ebbing tides turn, and Longleaf thrive.

Photograph Credits

Photographs listed in order:

Longleaf Resources

Print Resources:

Bartram, William. *The Travels of William Bartram.* 1791. Reprint, Naturalist's Edition, edited by Francis Harper. Athens: University of Georgia, 1998.

Earley, Lawrence S. *Looking for Longleaf: the fall and rise of an American forest.* Chapel Hill: The University of North Carolina Press, 2004.

Finch, Bill, Beth Maynor Young, Rhett Johnson, and John C. Hall. *Longleaf, far as the eye can see: a new vision of North America's richest forest.* Chapel Hill: The University of North Carolina Press, 2012.

Ray, Janisse. *Ecology of a Cracker Childhood.* Minneapolis: Milkweed Editions, 1999.

Online Resources:

The Longleaf Alliance	www.longleafalliance.org
The Nature Conservancy	www.nature.org
William Bartram Trail	www.bartramtrailconference.wildapricot.org
Defenders of Wildlife	www.defenders.org
National Audubon Society	www.audubon.org
Florida Fish and Wildlife Conservation	http://myfwc.com

About the Author

Frances Sankey Kwiatkowski grew up on a farm in rural northeast Georgia near the small town of Washington. She now lives with her family, dogs, cats, and horses near the lovely college town of Athens, Georgia. Her lifetime loves of nature, books, woodpeckers, and pitcher plants grew into this book.

www.kingdomoflongleaf.weebly.com

CPSIA information can be obtained
at www.ICGtesting.com
Printed in the USA
LVIC06n0313260116
472031LV00001B/2

9780692590607